Research Ate My Brain

THE PANIC-PROOF GUIDE TO SURVIVING HOMEWORK

TORONTO PUBLIC LIBRARY
ART BY MARTHA NEWBIGGING

ANNICK PRESS LTD.

Toronto • New York • Vancouver

We acknowledge the support of the Canada Council for the Arts, the Ontario
Arts Council, and the Government of Canada through the Book Publishing
Industry Development Program (BPIDP) for our publishing activities.

Cataloging in Publication

Research ate my brain : the panic-proof guide to surviving homework /
Toronto Public Library ; art by Martha Newbigging.

Includes bibliographical references and index.
ISBN 1-55037-939-9 (bound).—ISBN 1-55037-938-0 (pbk.)

    1. Homework—Handbooks, manuals, etc. 2. Research—Methodology—
Handbooks, manuals, etc. I. Newbigging, Martha II. Toronto Public Library

LB1048.R48 2005   371.3'028'1   C2005-902816-5

The text was typeset in Galliard.

Distributed in Canada by: Published in the U.S.A. by Annick Press (U.S.) Ltd.
Firefly Books Ltd.   Distributed in the U.S.A. by:
66 Leek Crescent   Firefly Books (U.S.) Inc.
Richmond Hill, ON   P.O. Box 1338
L4B 1H1   Ellicott Station
    Buffalo, NY 14205

Printed and bound in Canada by Friesens, Altona, Manitoba.

Visit us at: www.annickpress.com

• •

With special thanks to Ab. Velasco.
• •

In *Research Ate My Brain*, you will find a list of recommended websites
for research. With the exception of RAMP, Science Net, and Virtual
Reference Library, these websites are not endorsed by Annick Press or
Toronto Public Library.

    Also, please note that although these websites were current and
functional when this book went to press, Web addresses do change all
the time. If you come across a dead link, try typing just the first part of
the address – up to the first slash (/) – where applicable. This takes
you to the site host's home page.

Contents

To download worksheets for creating a work plan, organizing your note-taking, a standard essay outline, and checklists for written and oral assignments, go to www.annickpress.com.

foreword

When Annick Press approached the Toronto Public Library about collaborating on a book for teens about how to research, it was a perfect fit.

Responding to the complex yet interesting needs of youth is a priority for the Library. Since the Library opened in 1884, users have benefited from free access to up-to-date resources. Today, the Library has also adapted to the fast-paced Internet age. We currently provide access to over 140 research databases. The Library also offers free Internet classes on topics like online searching and homework help. In fact, it is these Internet classes that inspired Annick Press to create this book.

In the process of completing this book, the Library held focus groups with teens. We observed that most students possessed limited knowledge about conducting effective and efficient information searches. For instance, while students use search engines a lot, they seldom use – or know about – other tools like journals, subject directories, and databases.

Research Ate My Brain synthesizes the best resources offered by the Toronto Public Library as well as libraries around the world and the Internet. We aimed to produce a book that is both practical and relevant to today's students. While the tone will engage younger students, the information is just as useful for older students and adults.

Sir Francis Bacon once said that knowledge is power. In this book, students will learn how to access that power and how to use it to complete stellar projects.

—Josephine Bryant
City Librarian, Toronto Public Library

Introduction

BRAIN STRAIN!

You've had two months to complete your research project. It's 1 a.m. Candy wrappers cover the floor and you're jumping off the walls from a sugar buzz. You and your friends' instant-messaging names are alike: "I'm gonna die!" ... "Project due in 7 hrs!" ... You count down to the deadline throughout the night.

Sound familiar?

The hardest part of a research project can be getting started. It's much easier to procrastinate. And doing research can be a pain. Your teacher wants you to go to the library, but the Internet is so convenient – a giant pool of information, though who creates that info, or how reliable it is, you can't really be sure. So, where do you start? At the library catalog? You've searched the Net and got thousands of hits, and the few you've checked out looked pretty suspect. You need a road map to the right stuff.

Research Ate My Brain shows you how to track down the best information for school research projects. It's a refresher on the incredible resources you'll discover in any library – magazines, newspaper archives, books, videos, databases, unique collections – and it shows you how to find what you need in them, fast. You'll also learn new ways to use the Internet's powerful search tools and how to access library resources online. You'll find strategies to help you figure out what's good info and what's not, time-saving tips, and loads of helpful research websites. Once you've learned solid research skills, you'll use them over and over in future projects. And you know there will be plenty of those.

Still not sure where to start? No problem. Our first (short) chapter begins with ... how to start.

—Ab. Velasco
Author, Toronto Public Library

Chapter 1

The Dummy•Proof Work Plan

STAGE 1
CREATE YOUR MASTER PLAN

A work plan keeps you focused. You create a checklist of all the steps for your project and map out how and when you should finish each step. If this sounds as exciting as reading the phonebook, think of how nice it'll be when you don't have to blow away an entire weekend to play catch-up. Here's what you do:

Identify the task – Your teacher will tell you what he or she is looking for. Ask for help right away if you have questions.

Set a timeline – List all the things you have to do – research, rough draft, editing, final draft – along with deadlines for each.

STAGE 2
FIND THE INFORMATION

There is so much information out there, you don't have to worry about dead ends. Go to the library and the Internet to find information from a lot of different sources – books, magazines, journals, CDs, DVDs, search engines, databases, etc. In chapters 2 to 4 we'll show you how to use these resources.

1,000,000 TOPICS. 1,000,000 CHOICES

You will be assigned different types of research assignments. The possibilities to create fun and super projects are endless. So how creative do you want to get?

Field Report – You go to one or more places, collect data (through interviews, observations) and then write a report. For example, you go on a class trip to a TV newsroom, interview reporters, editors and producers, and then report how news stories are selected for broadcast.

Persuasive Essay – You develop a logical debate or argument using research data and your analysis. Have you thought about writing an essay examining why the number of young people who vote during elections has been historically low?

Oral Presentation– You present a topic verbally, using visual tools, like photos or PowerPoint. In a presentation for business class on advertising techniques and tactics, you show examples and analyze the best, worst, and most manipulative ads.

Profile – You research the history of a person or group focusing on major events, like a profile of music legend Bob Marley and his influence on modern music.

Lab Report – You perform experiments. Your report then includes your observations and conclusions. For example, you cut open and examine a rat's insides for a science report.

Research Report – You summarize available information on a topic. For example, you report on steroid use among some athletes competing in the Olympics.

Seminar – You come to class prepared with notes and discussion questions. You then teach a topic to your classmates. For example, you lead a seminar on teen pregnancy for health class.

As you look for information, keep in mind the following:

You may first find things that are not as helpful before you get to things that are.

Is it what you need? In Chapter 5 you'll learn how to evaluate sources and information.

Don't overdo it. You can always go back for more.

Some of your projects might cover one or more sub-topics. For example, sub-topics for vampires include history, famous vampires, and real-life vampires.

Can't find enough stuff for one sub-topic? Don't panic.

Expand on another sub-topic – for example, discuss famous vampires in several sections: TV vampires, movie vampires, and vampires in books.

Combine weak sub-topics together – Stuck? Combine TV, movie, and storybook vampires into one section.

STAGE 3
GOOD INFO IN, BAD INFO OUT

Taking good notes makes it easier for you when you start your draft. Try this shortcut: Use each source's title as a heading and include the page numbers as you take notes. This makes citing sources later a lot easier.

Here are other tips for effective note-taking:

Be selective – Skim your reading and take only the material that relates to your topics.

IS THIS YOU?
COMMON TEEN RESEARCH HABITS

1. You like to spend the least amount of effort possible on an assignment. Hello, you have more important things to do.

2. Planning ahead feels like a chore. Panicking for time near a deadline feels like second nature.

3. Does this comment apply to you? "Why get out of my pajamas to go to the library when I can find a source that is somewhat decent at home?"

4. When you find a few sources that you think are useful, you stop looking for more. Why make things complicated?

5. You don't spend a lot of time verifying the accuracy of your sources.

6. If you find one useful source, you will likely go to it first for future projects as opposed to looking for more appropriate sources.

Analysis: Did you agree to three or more of the above statements? No worries. All you need is this book and you will soon turn your life around!

- -

Summarize and paraphrase – Don't copy information word for word. Use point-form notes to summarize information in your words.

Keep track of quotes – Important quotes should be copied between quotation marks. Mark down who said it and the source you got it from.

STAGE 4
THE DRAFT: TAKE ONE

Create an outline before you start your first draft. It helps organize your topics and thoughts. Then fill out your outline with your notes.

Your teacher will often help you create a project outline. It usually consists of:

Introduction – Start with a bang. Use a catchy story, quote, or fact to hook your audience instantly.

Body – The body contains the main points of your project organized by sections of sub-topics or themes.

Conclusion – Finish with a statement or thought that rocks people's world. Okay, maybe that's a bit dramatic, but you get what we mean.

STAGE 5
EDIT, EDIT, EDIT

Chill out for a day before you make changes to your draft. Then look at it again with fresh eyes.

Nothing's perfect on the first try. You may have to give it a few shots before you get the best result. Ask someone – friend, parent, or teacher – to look at your draft and make suggestions.

As you edit, pay attention to the following:

What are the strengths? – What parts stand out? Bring them out more.

Weaknesses? – Do you need to do more research?

Move things around – Which sections work better somewhere else?

Cut – Take out the weak parts and let the good stuff stand out. Keep in mind the length requirement your teacher sets.

Be yourself – Read your work out loud. Trash parts that don't sound like you. Avoid using big words to sound smart because you may not end up communicating clearly.

Save your drafts regularly if you are using a word processor. Save your revisions with a different file name, so you can still look at the rough draft if you need to.

STAGE 6
UNVEIL YOUR MASTERPIECE

Do an inspection before you hand in your final draft.

Spelling – Do a computer spell-check, then read it over for mistakes that spell-check doesn't catch (for example, *there* instead of *their*; proper nouns).

Grammar and punctuation – You may lose marks for mistakes – even if it's not an English paper.

Double-check your facts – In chapter 5, you'll learn how to be sure the information you find is reliable. But you should also double-check key facts: names, dates, countries.

Citing sources – Give credit to the sources you used. In Chapter 6, we tell you why you should do this and how.

Presentation – Do you need a cover page, table of contents, or diagrams?

WE'RE HERE TO INSPECT THE FINAL DRAFT.

**ENOUGH PLANNING, ALREADY.
LET'S START THE PROJECT!**

So you see, when you break your projects into small pieces, they don't bite as much. And, as you know, when one project ends, a new one is never far behind. With experience and feedback, you'll learn what rocked and what bombed. You'll only get better.

In the next chapters, you'll learn how to use the resources at the library and on the Internet to find the best information for your projects. So, let's get started.

Chapter 2

Libraries: Project Parts Under One Roof

Did you recognize yourself in the last chapter's quiz? Here's
your first step to rehabilitation: Check out the library. You
need to find information – the best stuff – for your project.
Sure, the Internet is fast and easy. But using it alone means
that you miss out on a lot of the useful, free information
you'll find when you walk into a library: magazines and
academic journals, old newspaper archives, great books, books
that explain the great books, videos, DVDs, CDs, and more.

Never had a library card?
Think of it as your all-access pass. You usually just
need to show valid ID and you'll get your card free.
Then you can use the library's resources in the library
or from anywhere with Internet access (more on this in
Chapter 4). Some cards let you make photocopies too. Just charge
money to your card and slide it into a machine's card reader.

NAVIGATE WITH THE LIBRARY MAP

Use the computer catalog to find library materials. Libraries
that belong to a system of libraries catalog materials from all
branches. For example, the Chicago Public Library's catalog
lets you search from all of its 79 locations.

START WITH BASIC SEARCHES

Use the catalog to perform basic searches. Remember, spelling counts.

Search by author by typing in the last and/or first name.

Search by title by typing in the title of an item.

Search by subject by typing in a subject name.

PLACE LIMITS

When looking for specific types of items, use limits to narrow your search.

Limit by format – book, DVD, etc. – for specific types of items.

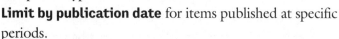

Limit by publication date for items published at specific periods.

Limit by language for items in specific languages.

Limit by location for items from a specific library.

EVALUATE SEARCH RESULTS

Your results are displayed alphabetically. When you click on each item, it lists the item record. This will include details like:

Availability – Is it available at the present or another library?

Call number – Where is it found on the shelf? (More on this on page 28.)

Item format – Is it a book, CD, DVD, etc.?

Number of copies – How many copies does the library have?

Publication date – When was it published?

Publisher – Who published it?

You can't sign out *closed-reference* materials. This will be indicated on the item's spine or cover and in the library catalog. Don't get bummed out though. You can still use them in the library. If it's a print item, photocopy the pages you need. If it's an audio or video item, ask a librarian about using a playing device.

THE PROJECT PARTS

Now that you know how to use the catalog, you can use it to quickly search through the library's resources.

FICTION BOOKS

Mystery novels, epic science-fiction and fantasy trilogies, or horror stories: these are some examples of fiction. In school, you read fiction for book reports. You also read it to learn about an author, setting, or theme (for example, racism in the American south of the 1930s in *To Kill a Mockingbird*).

NON-FICTION BOOKS

Biographies, UFO conspiracy theories, or strategy guides to video games: these are all examples of non-fiction. You read non-fiction books for facts, reviews, or analysis. Then you can use the information to write a report, essay, or profile.

Looking for hot reads? Look for or ask librarians about displays or reading lists. These list books such as Top 100 books for teens or award-winning books. You can also often find newspaper or magazine best-seller lists and reviews posted on bulletin boards.

REFERENCE BOOKS

Need a fast and easy starting point? Reference books give you the main points of a topic. There are different types:

Almanacs – Look for articles or lists about various topics.

Atlases – Look for maps and regional facts.

Bibliographies – Look for lists of related publications.

Dictionaries – Look it up: definitions, pronunciation, spelling, and more.

Directories – Look up names, addresses or phone numbers.

Encyclopedias – Look for articles and photos. These books are published in volumes and list topics alphabetically.

HOW AM I SUPPOSED TO FIND ANYTHING IN THIS MAZE? IT'D BE SO MUCH SIMPLER TO DO A FAST SEARCH ONLINE.

HI THERE. CAN I HELP YOU?

IS THIS YOUR FIRST VISIT TO THE LIBRARY?

NO, BUT I DON'T COME HERE MUCH ANYMORE SINCE WE GOT HIGH-SPEED AT HOME.

WELL, LET'S START WITH A NEW LIBRARY CARD.

Gazetteers – Look for geographical information.
Statistics books – Look for numerical data like population or economic resources.
Thesauruses – Look up synonyms and antonyms of words.

AUDIO-VISUAL MATERIALS

Audio-visual materials include videos, DVDs, cassettes, CDs, CD-ROMs and audio books. In school, you probably watch movies and have to write reviews. Most of the time, we just

PRIMARY VS. SECONDARY SOURCES

Your teacher will often tell you the number of sources you need to use and what those sources have to include (for example, books, articles, websites, etc.).

Primary sources are written or created as an event happens. They contain firsthand (personal) observations. A famous example is Anne Frank's *Diary of a Young Girl*, which was written during the Holocaust.

Secondary sources are written some time after an event has occurred. They contain information found in primary sources. So a book, article, or website that analyzes information from *The Diary of a Young Girl* is a secondary source.

Here are examples of both:

PRIMARY SOURCE	SECONDARY SOURCE
novels	textbooks, encyclopedias
poems, artwork, films, songs	analysis, reviews, criticisms
diaries and journals	works using facts from diary/journal
autobiographies	biographies (most)
newspaper articles (most)	magazine articles (most)
original scientific research	research interpretations
letters and e-mails	works using facts from letter/e-mail
interview transcripts	articles using facts from an interview
pictures and maps	

use these for entertainment. Popcorn, anyone? But even your favorite DVD (*Lord of the Rings, Star Wars*) can give you gold. Most movie DVDs have extras like behind-the-scenes footage and interviews.

Libraries carry current and older titles that might be out of stock at retail or rental stores. So, unless you want to own a copy, look at your library first.

NEWSPAPERS
What's your favorite section of the paper? Yeah, we like the comics and movie reviews, too.

You also read papers to find current information, photos, and opinions. Libraries keep local newspapers and some also have papers from other places.

You can also search for past issues, which are kept in archives. Older articles provide amazing historical information. Did you know that some larger libraries have archives dating back hundreds of years?

MICROFILM
Have you ever read a mystery novel or watched a program where the crime solver is reading a newspaper on a large screen? Since newspapers break down over time, older issues are usually transferred onto microfilm. These are reels of film of printed materials photographed at a reduced size. You use a microfilm reader to magnify the film onto a screen.

PERIODICALS – MAGAZINES
A periodical is published at periods of more than a day, such as weekly, monthly, or annually. Libraries keep current and back issues of periodicals. Older issues are often compiled into volumes, such as *National Geographic*. Like newspapers, periodicals are a good source for current and past articles.

A magazine is a periodical aimed at a general audience.

It usually has a shiny, flashy cover. You will find articles on current and popular topics as well as lots of photos and ads. Some popular titles include *Electronic Gaming Monthly*, *Spin*, and *Teen People*.

PERIODICALS – JOURNALS

A journal is a periodical aimed at an academic audience. It has a plain and serious cover, with titles that often include the words journal, review, or bulletin. Yes, a corpse sounds more lively than this. But journals are superb for research. Why? In them, you will find articles written and peer-reviewed by experts. For example, a 2003 article in *The American Journal of Sports Medicine* examined injury rates for female hockey players in comparison to male players.

INDEX

To find information in a book, newspaper, or periodical, use an index – an alphabetical list that directs you to topics in a source. **Print indexes** point you to information in other sources. They're arranged by author or subject headings. They list citations you can use to find sources, including author or title.

A newspaper index lists and points to newspaper articles.

A periodical index lists and points to articles from magazines.

A subject index lists and points to articles from journals.

Check out the index at the back of any non-fiction book (even this one): It lists names and subject topics and the page numbers that are found in the book. Look at a book's index first. If the topic you are researching is not listed a lot, then the book might not be useful to you.

EBOOKS

Electronic books – eBooks – are books available in the digital format. You can download them into your computer or an

eBook reader. Many libraries today allow users to borrow an eBook reader. Users can then choose from a list of eBook titles to download onto the reader. Most eBook readers can carry 10 or more titles at once.

You read an eBook on an eBook reader as you would a novel, except the text appears on a screen. You also get to play around with some cool features: for example, bookmark pages or search the contents of any book you've downloaded.

MULTILINGUAL COLLECTIONS

Have to write a book report for French or Spanish class? If you can read in another language, take a look at multilingual collections – items in other languages. You can find more information or different ways of looking at a topic.

WHERE THE HECK IS IT?

Library items are organized by a classification system. Items belonging to the same subject are grouped together. Each item has a call number – consisting of numbers and letters – labeled on the item's spine or cover. Think of a call number as a code to help you find items on the shelf.

The library catalog gives you the item's call number. Items are shelved in ascending order – numerical and/or alphabetical – based on the call number.

For example, *Surfing: Basic Techniques* by Arnold Madison has the call number 797.17 M. *797.17* stands for the subject and *M* stands for the author's last name.

The two widely used classification systems are the Dewey Decimal System and the Library of Congress System.

HOW DO YOU DEW?

WHAT IF IT'S NOT THERE?

Reserve Materials – Do you need to borrow an item that has been signed out or is only available at another branch?

Use the reserves system to place a hold on that item. You will be put on a waiting list and notified when it's available.

Interlibrary Loans (Interloans) – When an item is only available at another library system – in another city or country – ask your librarian if you can order it. These items are called interloans. You may be charged a fee, but the information might be worth it.

A bit of advice: Start your projects early in case you need to order material from the library. It never fails that if you wait till the last minute, someone else has borrowed the book or video that you need.

DIFFERENT LIBRARIES – DIFFERENT RESULTS

You may already be familiar with your local library, but it's worth exploring the different libraries in your community. Each library has its strengths and weaknesses. Some also have special collections containing historical artifacts that you can't find anywhere else.

School Library – A good place to start your research, because it is close by. Still, the resources may be limited, especially when everyone in your class is doing similar projects.

Public Library – You visit public libraries to use a collection that meets the needs of your community. Some communities have several libraries that are connected in a system. Each one allows you to use resources available from the entire system.

Academic Library – Academic libraries – in universities, colleges, and research associations – offer academic resources,

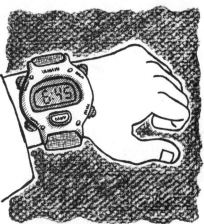

archives, and special collections. For college and university libraries, you need to be a student enrolled in that school to have free full access. If not, you have to pay a user fee.

Special Library – A collection that deals with specific subjects, usually maintained by individuals, companies, or research organizations. Some special libraries, such as company ones, or those owned by newspapers or TV news networks, can only be used by specific groups of people, such as employees. You may need a personal connection to get access to some of these.

National Library – You visit a national library, maintained by a country's government, to use a collection that preserves the nation's history. These collections are usually closed-reference. (We show you how to find national library websites on page 73.)

When university student Amy, 18, was in high school, she used an effective method to organize her notes. She first listed all her project's topics. "I then went through the notes and gave them a letter based on which topic they fit into. I labeled them 'misc.' when I couldn't figure out which topic they belonged to. Then I cut them up and placed information belonging to the same topic together," she says. This method lets you see which topics are strong or weak. For weaker sections, go back and do more research.

NOW YOU CAN GO ONLINE

So, isn't it worth rolling out of bed to go to the library? Still, as you will see, the Internet has changed the way students research. In Chapter 3, you'll learn reliable search techniques to find info on the Net. Most libraries are also connected to the Internet and in Chapter 4 you'll discover how to access much of their information with the click of a mouse.

Chapter 3
Searching in Cyberspace

For history class, you have to research the life of a famous figure, like Nelson Mandela or Oprah Winfrey, and present the information as a graphic novel. Before you map out your storyboards, you need the facts.

Do you click on Google or some other search engine? In a snap you will find millions of websites. But which should you visit? And, what's more, the Internet is unregulated. There are no rules that decide who can create a website. So, yes, there are a lot of websites. But not all of them are reliable. Or free.

So how do you find the best stuff on the Net?

SEARCH ENGINES – UNIVERSES OF WEBSITES

Use a search engine, like Yahoo! (www.yahoo.com), to find websites devoted to specific topics. Athletes? Dance moves? Health topics you're embarrassed to talk about? Done.

Type in the search engine's Web address in the address bar. This takes you to its home page. Locate the search box and then type in keywords relating to what you are searching for. Then results (hits) – based on your keywords – are displayed as a list of websites.

The websites listed in this book are not necessarily endorsed by the publisher or the Toronto Public Library.

Here's the catch, though: search engines contain uneval-uated Web pages. So you get the good and the bad. That's why it's important to evaluate these sources, which you'll learn to do in Chapter 5.

DON'T USE JUST ONE

Every search engine works differently. Some even let you search for images, audio, video, or articles. Take a look at different ones to see what's available. Some to try: **Altavista** (www.altavista.com), **Google** (www.google.com), **Lycos** (www.lycos.com), **MSN Search** (search.msn.com)

MULTI-SEARCHES WITH ONE CLICK

Use a metasearch engine to do preliminary research. It searches through several search engines at once and blends the results together. It gives an overview of what is available on your topic.

You can also use a metasearch engine when a regular search engine isn't helpful. Some to try: **Dogpile** (www.dogpile.com), **Ixquick** (www.ixquick.com), **Mamma** (www.mamma.com), **Vivisimo** (www.vivisimo.com)

SURFING WEBSITES 101

You use a browser – like Internet Explorer or Netscape – to view websites. The main page of a website is called the home page. The secondary pages and sections are called Web pages.

On the browser's address bar, type in a Web address (also called a URL) to go to a website. You can also go to websites by clicking on a link.

Every website is set up differently. Explore what each site has to offer. Here are some common features you will find.

"About Us" – This section gives you information about the individual or organization that created the site. Do they look legitimate?

Search box – Some sites have built-in search boxes that let you find information within the site. Use it to do quick searches.

Site index – It lists alphabetically and links to sections within the site. Use it to quickly find the information you need.

FAQ – (Frequently Asked Questions) This lists popular questions and answers about the site.

Help buttons – Can't find something? Look for help links. These let you e-mail questions to the people who manage the site.

Links – When you find one website helpful, browse through their links to look for more websites.

HOW TO GET THE BEST RESULTS

Every search engine works differently. Still, you can use similar techniques to find the best results. The key is to explore and experiment.

1. IDENTIFY YOUR SEARCH TERMS

What is the question you are trying to answer? Identify the main concepts in your topic. Then brainstorm a list of search terms. Use terms or short phrases, instead of sentences or questions. Keep in mind the following:

Use the correct spelling.

Use specific nouns or objects as search terms.

Team Jenny Finds the Right Stuff

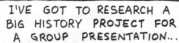

Use no more than eight terms, to avoid overly broad results.
Use synonyms and variations if you're not sure of exact terms.
Use lower-case letters to search for both lower- and upper-case terms.

2. USE SPECIAL SEARCH FEATURES

Most search engines allow you to use special features to improve your search.

Quotation marks – Put a term or phrase in "quotation marks" to find exact phrases. This is helpful if you are searching for names or titles (for example, "Alicia Keys" or "Romeo and Juliet").

Boolean searching – The Boolean search is named after George Boole, a famous English mathematician. It involves using the words AND, OR, NOT – called Boolean operators – between your search terms. These operators create a relationship between your search terms (see below). Boolean operators help narrow or broaden results. Be sure to capitalize them.
AND – Results with all terms included (for example, basketball AND team)
OR – Results with either term included (for example, America OR U.S.A.)
NOT – Results exclude terms after NOT (for example, music NOT country)

Wildcard symbols –Use wildcard symbols when you don't know the exact term or how to spell it. Here are two examples:
Use the question mark (?) to match one character in the place of a letter or symbol (for example, wom?n finds woman, women).

Use the asterisk (*) in place of sequences of letters. Depending on the search tool, place it at the beginning, end, or both ends of the term (for example, teen* finds teen, teenager, teenagers; *berry finds blueberry, raspberry, etc.).

Word math – If you find Boolean searching a bit complicated, try a little word math instead.

Addition – Use the plus (+) symbol to add. Your results will include all the words in your search. Don't put spaces between words and symbols. Example: *+Basketball+Lakers*.

Subtraction – Use the minus (–) symbol to subtract. Your results will include pages that do not mention the words you have subtracted. Example: *music–country*.

3. TRY AN ADVANCED SEARCH

Click on the advanced search link (or similar phrase) on the home page of a search engine. Use the different limits offered, for example, language, date, etc., to narrow your search.

TIMESAVER TIP

Most schools, colleges and universities, governments, TV networks or programs, and other traditional sources have their own websites. Use a search engine to find them and explore what information and links they offer.

4. REFINE YOUR RESULTS

Do you need to broaden your search? Or do you want to narrow down the results?

Use synonyms or variations of the term to broaden your search. For example, if you're searching for information on "atomic bombs," you might also try "nuclear warfare" or "nuclear weapons."

Most search engines allow you to search within your results – by clicking on a link – to find narrower results. For example, after searching "nuclear weapons," you can then search within the results for "Hiroshima."

5. TRY AND TRY AGAIN

You might have to refine your search several times. That's okay, because you'll find better stuff that way. You can also use different search engines and metasearch engines. Or you can use a subject directory (see the next section).

FROM THE LAB TO YOUR HOME: A BRIEF INTERNET TIMELINE

1969 Concerned about nuclear warfare, the U.S. Department of Defense, through its Advanced Research Projects Agency (ARPA), establishes ARPANET, a network that links university and military computers.

1988 A commercial e-mail service is linked to the Internet – the first connection outside the research community.

1991 The World Wide Web – developed by British computer scientist Tim Berners-Lee – becomes part of the Internet.

SIR TIM

2000 360 million people around the world (6 per cent of the world population) have Internet access.

2010? Half of the world population is expected to have some form of Internet access.

TIMESAVER TIP

Use the "find" function on your keyboard (CTRL-F) to locate a word or phrase within an electronic document. This takes you right to the information you need. For example, if you are reading a 20-page document on stem-cell research, you can use this function to pinpoint when the phrase "embryonic stem cells" appears.

SUBJECT DIRECTORIES – EXPERT-APPROVED WEBSITES

Use a subject directory to find websites about a broad or easily defined subject like piracy, poetry, or pollution. You browse a subject index or do keyword searches to find websites.

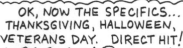

I KNOW... I'LL DO A COMPARISON OF HOW WE COMMEMORATE NOVEMBER 11TH TO WHAT THEY DO IN UNCLE PETE'S HALIFAX.

THERE WAS A GOOD STORY IN OUR LOCAL NEWSPAPER YESTERDAY, BUT I PITCHED IT.

NO PROBLEM, DAD. I CAN GET THAT ARTICLE OFF THE NEWSPAPER'S OWN WEBSITE.

THE CHALLENGE WILL BE FINDING AN ARTICLE FROM A PUBLICATION IN HALIFAX.

I'D BETTER CHECK A NEWS DIRECTORY SITE.

COOL. HERE'S A LINK TO THE HALIFAX DAILY NEWS... AND COVERAGE OF UPCOMING EVENTS FOR REMEMBRANCE DAY.

Halifax Daily News NOV. 2, 20c

FINANCE SPORTS ARTS

REMEMBRANCE DAY AT THE CITADEL

EVEN BETTER. THIS SITE WILL LET ME DOWNLOAD THE ARTICLE FOR FREE.

TO: IRENE@CENTRALHIGH.E
EVE@CENTRALHIGH.EDU
SUBJECT: NOV. 11 PROJECT
HI GALS,
THIS IS WHAT I'VE GOT
SO FAR

NOW I'LL SEND THESE TWO STORIES TO EVE AND IRENE.

DINNNERRRR!

Unlike search engines, which are built by a computer program, subject directories are built by experts, like librarians. This means that the websites you'll find are more reliable. The Virtual Reference Library (www.virtualreference library.ca) is a directory created by the Toronto Public Library with a focus on Canadian content. About (www.about.com) is a directory of articles written by expert guides; for example, the site's table-tennis guide is a two-time Olympian.

Here are some other recommended subject directories.

Academic Info (www.academicinfo.net)

Awesome Library (www.awesomelibrary.org)

Infomine (www.infomine.ucr.edu)

Internet Public Library (www.ipl.org)

Librarians' Index to the Internet (www.lii.org)

Looksmart (www.looksmart.com)

HOW TO USE SUBJECT DIRECTORIES

Use similar techniques to those you would use for search engines. Here's what else you need to know.

BROWSE THE SUBJECT INDEX

Subject directories organize websites into broad subject categories. They then branch off into narrower categories.

Locate and use the directory's subject index. It alphabetically lists links to broad categories. Click on one and you will find a list of narrower topics, and so on. You eventually end up with a list of websites about very specific topics.

For example, on the subject directory Looksmart, you might click on Society and Politics (broad category). This takes you to narrower topics like Crime and Justice, Law, and Social Science. If you click on Law, you can then click onto Branches of Law and then Civil Rights and then International Human Rights. Here you'll find case histories, convention texts and publications dedicated to fundamental human rights.

DO SUBJECT SEARCHES

Use broad search terms – like aerospace engineering, animal behavior or artificial intelligence – since subject directories organize websites by subject. Most directories have built-in search engines that let you search for sites that way. Experiment with the search features you learned in the previous section (Boolean, etc.) to see which you can use here.

EVALUATE RESULTS

Search engines usually include text from websites in the results. Subject directories, on the other hand, create their own useful summary. Look for the **breadcrumb trail** – think Hansel and Gretel minus the witch – often included in the description. It lists the paths of categories you click through to get to each site. You can click on any category to find a list of other websites.

Here's an example of a breadcrumb trail: **Society and Politics – Law – Branches of Law – Civil Rights – International Human Rights.**

FIND THE DEEP WEB

Think you can find everything on the Internet? Have you heard of the deep Web?

The deep Web is the part of the Internet that most common search engines can't or don't access. Some refer to it as the Invisible Web. It does sound like something from a sci-fi movie, but it's really quite simple.

Think of it this way: the visible Web contains static Web pages, meaning they have a fixed Web address. The deep Web contains dynamic pages (pages that do not have fixed Web addresses), which are created by individual searches. These Web pages include high-quality online journal articles, found in online databases. So if you're looking for journal articles for a persuasive essay about genetically modified foods, you might have some luck searching in the deep Web.

WHY DOES IT EXIST?

Don't get us wrong: search engines are very useful. Many search engines now also include deep Web content in their search. But they miss out on most. Why?

Most search engines are designed to find static Web pages. **It is too expensive** to include all the complex pages found in the deep Web.

HOW TO FIND THE DEEP WEB

The good news is that there are now directories on the Internet that let you find the deep Web. Not everything is free, but it's worth checking out.

(www.completeplanet.com) – Find over 70,000-plus databases. (www.profusion.com) – You can set up a search alert, which e-mails you when one of your searches turns up new results. (www.invisible-web.net) – Links to mostly free databases.

READ ARTICLES ONLINE

Looking for news, magazine, or journal articles?

Use a search engine or subject directory to find the websites of news and academic organizations.

Use a news directory. For example, NewsDirectory.com (www.newsd.com) lets you find U.S. and Canadian news and magazine websites by area code. Then look for international websites by using an index.

Use the "Articles" search function available on some search engines and subject directories. For example, Looksmart's "Articles" tab lets you find over 5.5 million articles from 900 titles.

Use a deep Web directory to find online databases. You might find that many websites charge a fee to use their

information, especially for older articles. What do you do? Find
out on pages 68 and 69.

Find people online
Looking for an address or phone number?
Use an online directory. For example, InfoSpace
(www.infospace.com) lets you search for people
all over the world. Try a search for yourself or your parents. Now
search by reverse look-up. Type in a phone number to find a
name. Cool, huh?

PLAY AROUND WITH MULTIMEDIA

You can find tons of image, audio, and video files on the
Web. These are all fun ways to spice up your projects.

Worth a thousand words – Find pictures or screenshots of
your favorite celebrity, manga/anime, or a famous painting
for an art-history class project.
You can use a regular search engine and include the
word *picture* – or other related term – in your search. Some
search engines have image-only search functions, including
Picsearch (www.picsearch.com), Yahoo!, and Google.

TAP INTO SOUND AND VIDEO

You can use a regular search engine to find audio and video
files – music videos, concerts, radio and TV clips, or famous
speeches like Martin Luther King's "I Have a Dream."
Simply include the type of file you're looking for in your
search (for example, "Hilary Duff"+"music video"). You can
also use search engines or services that let you do audio- or
video-only searches, such as:
AllTheWeb (www.alltheWeb.com),
Altavista (www.altavista.com)
Lycos Pictures and Sound (multimedia.lycos.com)

Post your research questions on the Net
Discussion forums are websites that work like bulletin boards. You can post, read, and respond to messages about specified topics. Use a search engine to find them (for example, +astronomy+ "discussion forum"). Be wary: Anyone can post on a forum, so the information isn't always reliable, but there are many that are created by experts, like schools and libraries.

PLUGGING IN

Ever been on a website when a box popped up and said you needed to install some software to view stuff?

Plug-ins are downloadable software that enhances your browser's function. They let you hear sound, watch video, or open special files. You will often be guided through the download and installation process. Sometimes you have to look for the plug-in. In this case, use a search engine.

Watch out for viruses that might harm your computer. Speak to your parents, staff at the computer store, or your Internet service provider about installing anti-virus software on your computer.

Here are some plug-ins you might use during your research.

Adobe Acrobat Reader (www.adobe.com/products/acrobat/readstep2.html) – Opens .pdf files.

Macromedia Shockwave Player (www.macromedia.com/shockwave/download) – Runs Flash movies.

Real Player (www.real.com/player/) – Opens Real Audio files.

Windows Media Player (www.microsoft.com/windows/windowsmedia/download/) – Opens a variety of files like .mp3, .avi, or .wav files.

Winzip (www.winzip.com/download) – Compresses one or more files into a .zip file.

From "In Flanders Fields" by John McCrae.

WHAT'S YOUR FAVORITE SITE?

Click on the icon marked **favorites** on your browser's tool-bar to save useful websites (like Hotmail or Discovery Channel's website) to the favorites folder. Visit these sites later by opening your favorites folder and clicking on the links.

Adding links to your favorites folder makes it easier to remember which online sources to cite later. You can also revisit these sites for future projects. To get you started, here are some of our favorites (below). A note: website addresses change constantly. If you find that an address doesn't work, try typing just the part before the first forward slash (/).

If you have a favorite research website, please let us know by e-mailing annickpress@annickpress.com. We will post them on www.annickpress.com.

GENERAL SUBJECTS

The Big 6 (www.big6.com/kids/7-12.htm) – Read and learn about the stages of projects, from starting a task, to finding and evaluating information.

Internet Public Library Teenspace (www.ipl.org/div/teen/browse/gh0000/) – Find websites for different school subjects, as well as ideas on writing a good paper.

Statistics Canada – Learning Resources (www.statcan.ca/english/edu/) – Statistics and census information. Learn how to collect and use statistical data.

Spark Notes (www.sparknotes.com) – Study notes on famous literary works and other school subjects that include summaries, definitions, and diagrams.

ENGLISH LITERATURE

Absolute Shakespeare (www.absoluteshakespeare.com) – Learn about Shakespeare's plays, poems, quotes, and sonnets, as well as his life.

CliffsNotes (www.cliffsnotes.com) – Read literature notes

STAYING SAFE FROM ONLINE PREDATO

Most teens today use the Internet to communicate – e-ma
instant messaging or chat – more than to do research. Do
In turn, the Internet has now become an ideal place for ch
predators, pedophiles, kidnappers, and even murderers.

How does this happen? The Internet allows users to
anonymous and false identities. So it is easier than it wou
real life for predators to lure their prey into face-to-face

"It is rarely random. An online predator will choose y
target and then lure you closer and closer," says Samant
Wilson, a former police officer, and founder of Kidproof
(www.kidproofcanada.com), a child-safety education or

If you feel unsafe in an online chat, exit the chat ro
away. Tell your parents, guardian, or a trusted adult wh
pened. Here are five more safety tips:

1. Protect your identity – Don't give out personal
your name, age, address, phone number, e-mail, schoc
or even sport's team. "Online predators can find little
information from several conversations and piece it a
and find you," Samantha says.

2. Stay in control – "Chatting on the Internet at ͻ
morning could be pretty romantic," says Samantha a
predators create such settings to gain access, privac
trol. Watch out for leading comments like "Are your
there?" or "Don't tell anyone about us."

3. Beware of emotional manipulation – Pred
that teens can often feel lonely, which makes them
manipulate. Beware of people who want to be you
seek to isolate you from loved ones. Keep your gu

4. Keep your parents in the know – Your par
guardian only want to keep you safe. "You do kno
computers than your parents," Samantha says. "\
show them how much you know?"

5. Don't meet online friends alone – Not e
Internet is dangerous. If you want to meet your
real life, take your parents or a trusted adult wit
friend in a public place.

online that provide detailed summary and analysis of popular books.

Novelguide (www.novelguide.com) – Provides analysis of literature including literature profiles, theme analysis, and author biographies.

Online Books Page (digital.library.upenn.edu/books) – Read hundreds of complete books, like Mark Twain's *The Adventures of Huckleberry Finn*. These books are available for free because they are either in the public domain – that is, the copyright has expired – or the copyright holder – usually the author – has given his or her permission.

Quoteland (www.quoteland.com) – Find quotations on many topics and identify the authors of famous quotes.

GEOGRAPHY

Country Reports (www.countryreports.org) – Profiles of over 260 countries; lists topics like 100 largest cities in the world, and capital cities.

Nations Online (www.nationsonline.org) – Find capital cities, population figures, flags, maps and official languages of countries around the world.

United Nations Cyberschoolbus (www.cyberschoolbus.un.org/infonation3) – Compare statistics for population, economy, environment, health and technology of up to six countries. Results displayed as a visual bar graph.

World Atlas (www.worldatlas.com) – Country atlases, flags, maps and more.

HISTORY

America's Library (www.americaslibrary.gov) – What did Abraham Lincoln have in his pocket the night he was assassinated? Find great historical trivia along with the hard facts in this history website created by the Library of Congress.

Exploring Ancient World Cultures (eawc.evansville.edu) –

Learn about the ancient cultures of China, Egypt, Greece, India, and many more.

Rulers (www.rulers.org) – Lists heads of state and heads of government for all countries and territories as far back as 1700.

dMarie Time Capsule (www.dmarie.com/timecap) – Enter an exact date to find out significant events that occurred. Create your own time capsule too!

World Heritage List (whc.unesco.org/pg.cfm?cid=31) – Provides historical information and photos of national treasures like Australia's Great Barrier Reef.

MATH

Ask Dr. Math (www.mathforum.org/dr.math) – Answers to common problems.

Math.com (www.math.com) – Learn and try sample questions on topics like fractions, exponents, and inequalities.

Online Conversion (www.onlineconversion.com) – Performs over 50,000 different conversions for over 5,000 different units.

Purple Math (www.purplemath.com) – Algebra lessons.

S.O.S Math (www.sosmath.com) – Advanced topics from algebra and calculus.

SCIENCE

Chemicool Periodic Table (www.chemicool.com) – Detailed information about chemical elements such as atomic number and weight.

Human Anatomy Online (www.innerbody.com) – A fun, interactive website about the human body that features animations and detailed descriptions.

The Physics Classroom (www.physicsclassroom.com) – Learn basic physics concepts and test your skills in tutorials.

Science in the Headlines (www.nationalacademies.org/headlines) – Over 2,500 research reports related to current topics like stem-cell research and HIV/AIDS.

Science Net (sciencenet.torontopubliclibrary.ca) – Search for websites about many science topics, including geology, paleontology, and zoology.

ENCYCLOPEDIAS

Encarta (encarta.msn.com) – More than 4,500 articles, Top 10 lists, quizzes, online math homework help, and more.

Encyclopedia.com (www.encyclopedia.com) – Over 55,000 articles from the Columbia Encyclopedia (6th edition), daily history trivia, and more.

Encyclopaedia Britannica (www.britannica.com) – Browse an index, use timelines, or read daily trivia. You need to pay a fee to have full access.

ALMANACS

Fact Monster (www.factmonster.com/almanacs.html) – Search for world news by year, do daily quizzes and games, get homework help, and more.

Information Please (www.infoplease.com) – Includes daily almanacs like "This Day in History," Word of the Day, multiple-choice quizzes, and famous birthdays.

DICTIONARIES

OneLook Dictionary Search (www.onelook.com)

Word Central (www.wordcentral.com)

THESAURUS

Merriam-Webster Online (www.m-w.com)

Roget's II: The New Thesaurus (www.bartleby.com/62)

LINKING BACK TO LIBRARIES

The Internet does have a lot of information, but some of it can be unreliable or cost money. Don't you have enough to worry about? Coming up next, we show you how heading back to the library solves these headaches.

EVE: I DID A NAME SEARCH ON A NURSE VET FROM JEN'S NEWS ARTICLE. THEN I CALLED HER UP AND NOW SHE IS COMING TO OUR CLASS NEXT WEEK.

IRENE: WAY TO GO!

JENNY: AWESOME. HER PERSONAL TESTIMONIAL IS GOING TO MAKE IT REAL TO EVERYONE.

GOING TO MAKE IT REAL TO EVERYONE.

IRENE: HEY, IF WE WANT TO PUT SOME EMOTIONAL IMPACT INTO THIS SHOW, CHECK THIS POEM RECORDING THAT I FOUND.

FF.WAV

CLICK

IN FLANDERS FIELDS THE POPPIES BLOW BETWEEN THE CROSSES, ROW ON ROW...

WHEW! THAT'S REALLY HEAVY, IRENE.

YEAH, I DIDN'T REALIZE A FEW GOOD WEBSITES COULD DELIVER LIKE THIS.

I THINK I'LL TRY TO WORK THIS INTO A SONG. YOU GUYS WANNA COME OVER?

YEAH, LET'S WRAP IT UP AT IRENE'S.

...AND THEN LET'S JAM!

Chapter 4

Libraries in Cyberspace

Have you ever searched through your family's entire magazine collection just to find a single article? Was that you digging through the recycling box for last week's newspaper? You really thought you could avoid making that trip to the library.

The good news is that most libraries around the world now have their own websites. You can use their online services for many tasks that once required you to visit the library — to use the library catalog, place items on reserve, even to find out if you have any fines.

You can also use the library's electronic tools, such as databases, which let you find items like newspaper or magazine articles a lot faster. You can tap into digitized collections, visit library websites created especially for teens, or e-mail a question to a librarian on the other side of the globe.

Doing research has never been this fast and easy.

DATABASES –
HITTING JACKPOTS OF INFORMATION

A database is an electronic collection of information that has been organized for easy searching. You use one to find electronic versions of items like newspaper, magazine, and journal articles.

You generally use a database to find up-to-date information, such as research studies, book reviews, or consumer-product reports. The information might be so new that it has not yet appeared in books.

In Chapter 2, you learned about print indexes. You found that using them could be a drag, because you have to search out articles one by one. Databases, which are electronic indexes, are much more powerful.

You can find several articles at once within seconds.
You can find articles from academic or popular, local or international sources.
You can print and e-mail articles.

WHY USE LIBRARY DATABASES?

Sure, there are databases on the Net, but the better ones often charge you a fee. As you learned in Chapter 3, most online search tools don't always find the best database articles either.

To quickly find the most reliable information, use your library's databases. They're free, too. You can also use some of them from home. Ask your librarian about how to do this, or snoop around on your library's website and find out for yourself.

HOW DATABASES WORK

Every database is set up differently, but they all work alike. Once you learn how to use one, it is easy to figure out how to use another. It's like riding a bike – almost. Here are some common things you will find on a database and how to use them.

Read the FAQ to learn about how the database works.
Click on the search tips link to learn how to improve your search.
Type in search terms in the search box to find articles.
Use an advanced search to limit your search and results.

OK, GET THIS SORRY PROJECT.

"YOU ARE A TOUR OPERATOR FOR WELLINGTON, ONTARIO. MAKE A BROCHURE THAT PROMOTES A LOCAL ATTRACTION. CONTRAST YOUR HOMETOWN WITH ONE LARGE CITY OF THE WORLD."

THAT'S SO EASY. COVER THE HISTORICAL SITES, ANTIQUE SHOPS AND THE U-PICK FARMS.

I WAS HOPING FOR SOMETHING MORE UNIQUE, MAYBE EVEN FUN.

WISH I COULD HELP BUT I'VE GOT A BUS TO CATCH. I'M SURE YOU'LL FIGURE IT OUT.

EASY FOR YOU TO SAY, MISS "I'M-SO-OUTTA-HERE."

Most databases provide a list of all the sources in their collection (for example, magazine titles). Use this list to help limit your search.

Lost? No worries. Look through the help page, use the e-mail help links, or ask a librarian for assistance.

HOW TO SEARCH DATABASES

Databases use an item record to describe each article in their collection. This record includes the citation (title, author, publication, date, etc.) and subject heading. You search for articles by using search terms or phrases. Your search term then looks for a match in the item record or in the article's text. It's almost like using a search engine.

Ready to search? Let's go.

1. IDENTIFY YOUR TOPIC AND TERMS

What is the research question you want to answer? Identify the key concepts and topics. Brainstorm a list of search terms, synonyms, and related terms that you can use. For example, if you are writing an essay analyzing shopping malls as a social phenomenon, you might use a *combination* of the following terms: shopping mall, shopping center, strip mall or mall, with social phenomenon, history, influence, trends, research, analysis, studies, influence, etc. One possible combination might be *shopping mall* AND *history*.

2. USE THE APPROPRIATE DATABASE

Are you looking for news articles about teen gangs or the dangers of monster parties? Or are you looking for journal articles about anorexia? After you identify your topic and the type of information you need, look for a database that best fits your topic. We discuss different databases in the next section (see page 67).

3. DO A BASIC SEARCH

There are three ways to use your search terms or phrases to find articles.

Keyword search – You find articles by matching your search term in the item record and/or the article's text.

Relevance search – This is a keyword search, except the articles in which your search term appears the most are listed in the results first.

Subject search – You find articles by matching your search term to the subject heading(s) that is included in the article's item record.

4. TRY SPECIAL SEARCH FEATURES

Most databases allow you to use quotation marks (" "), Boolean operators and wildcard symbols to improve your search. (See page 37 to refresh yourself on these.)

The proximity search is another neat trick you can play with. You use proximity operators between search terms.

W (within) – Finds articles that contain search terms within the number of words you specify and in that exact order. For example, *retro W/4 music* finds articles that contain those two words within four words of each other. *Retro* has to come before *music*.

N (next to) – Finds articles that contain search terms within the number of words specified but in any order. For example, *soccer N/3 tournament* finds articles that contain *soccer* and *tournament* within three words of each other and in any order.

Not all your search results will be useful. Mark each item that interests you by clicking on the box beside it. When you finish browsing, you can click on a link that says something like "View marked documents." A new page will load and list only the items you have marked.

5. USE AN ADVANCED SEARCH

Use limits in the database's advanced-search feature to narrow your search. Limits may include author, newspaper, magazine or journal name, type of article (for example, journal), or publication date.

Most databases allow you to choose from a list of options. For example, if you are using the "journal name" limit, you can browse through a complete list of titles. This makes your search more specific.

6. SORT YOUR RESULTS

The number of articles you find is listed at the top of the results page. Recent articles are listed at the top of your results. Most databases also allow you to list results the other way around. You can sometimes sort by relevance too. This means that articles in which your search term appears the most are listed first.

7. EVALUATE YOUR RESULTS

Each result will include the article's citation. It may also give a short summary and word count. The result will also show if the article is an abstract or full text.

Abstract – You get a short summary. In this case, find out if the library has a text copy or if it exists as full text in other databases.

Full text – You get the complete article, which may include photos.

8. REFINE

Are you not finding enough articles? Are your results too broad? Are you getting articles you don't understand? Use different search terms and limits — and search skills you learned in Chapter 3 — to broaden or narrow your search.

If you still don't find what you need, use a different database.

E-MAIL AND PRINT ARTICLES

Most databases allow you to e-mail articles. If you can, e-mail articles to yourself. You can then use them anytime from home or anywhere with Internet access.

To print an article, click on a printer-friendly version link. This version ensures that each article is completely printed.

CHOOSING THE BEST DATABASE

To give you an idea of what you can find on databases, we have listed some to explore in this section. You should also ask your librarian about the ones available at your library. Experiment with a few to find the best results.

SUBJECT-SPECIFIC

Are you looking for the latest journal articles on space exploration? Do you want the different viewpoints on controversial current events like global warming? More important, why did Ken and Barbie really break up? Wouldn't you like to know? Check out these examples:

ProQuest Research Library – Articles in the arts, humanities, social sciences, and more

Business and Company Resource Center –
Company profiles, annual reports, and industry profiles
NoveLIST – Need to find a good
book? Author biographies? Check
this out.
America: History and Life – U.S.
and Canadian history and culture
World History Online – Civilizations
and cultures from prehistoric times
through the modern era
Science Online – Most scientific
disciplines arranged by diagrams, definitions,
biographies, essays, experiments and timeline

NEWS

Sorting through inky stacks of papers or reels of microfilm
just to find one article sounds dry, doesn't it? Depending on
the database, you can find current and older articles much
faster. For example, ProQuest Newsstand lets you search
from over 350 U.S. and international newspapers, and
Canadian Newsstand from over 190 Canadian news sources.

MAGAZINES

Looking for articles about hot political issues? Interviews
with famous people? There's no need to raid your parents'
collections. Use a magazine database like the Canadian
Periodical Index, which lets you search for articles from
Canadian magazines, or the General Reference Center Gold,
for U.S. and international magazines.

Do you need to research a topic – like when a politician
won an election – but you don't know when it happened?
Use a reference source, like an encyclopedia, to find the
date or period. You can then limit your search by date.

GO DIGITAL

You can use digital collections to find current information or knowledge from centuries ago. Look on a library website's home page for a link to these. Items in these online collections – rare books, articles, photos, memorabilia, posters – are preserved by being scanned into an electronic (digitized) format. They may also include audio and video recordings.

You can find stuff like rarely seen Coca-Cola ads from the 1950s without looking through dusty shelves. One hundred years from now, a teen in the future (maybe your great-grandkids) can look at stuff from your time. Have you ever read online comics from publishers like Marvel Comics (www.marvel.com)? These are also examples of digitized items.

Using digital collections is like looking through a regular website. Some also work like a search engine, a subject directory, or both.

JUST HOW ANCIENT?

Digital collections vary in subject and size. Find out what's available and which ones are free. For example, the American Memory (memory.loc.gov/ammem/index.html) digital collections let you search from over 7.5 million items, like the Coca-Cola ads mentioned above, from the Library of Congress history collections.

DIGITIZING THE NEWS

You can use digital news collections to find 100-year-old articles. Many newspapers are converting their archives into an electronic format. Articles are scanned in their original form, including the pictures, ads, and obituaries. Did you know that the New York Times collection has over 15 million articles, from as far back as 1851? Ask your librarian about these collections and consider how you can use them. Why not look for an article that was printed the day you were born?

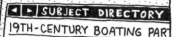

SUBJECT DIRECTORY

19TH-CENTURY BOATING PAR

LEAVING THE BUSTLE OF THE CITY BEHIND, FAMILIES AND FRIENDS WOULD LOAD UP DOZENS OF ROWBOATS, DEPART FROM WELLINGTON SHORES AND MAKE THEIR WAY ACROSS THE BAY TO PICNIC ALL DAY ON THE GRAND SAND DUNE BEACHES.

I THINK I CAN USE THIS BUT I WISH I HAD SOME PICTURES.

FOR THAT I'LL HAVE TO SHOW YOU THE GATEWAY.

YOU MEAN YOU'RE KICKING ME OUT?

HAH! ON THE CONTRARY, I'M LETTING YOU IN!

THIS GATEWAY, OR PORTAL, IS A DOORWAY TO ALL KINDS OF INFORMATION ABOUT OUR LOCAL HISTORY: ACTUAL NEWSPAPERS, JOURNALS AND PHOTOGRAPHS...

...YOU MAY EVEN FIND OLD YEAR-BOOKS FROM YOUR HIGH SCHOOL.

SOUNDS LIKE HOW "TEEN SPACE" WORKS. IS IT A PORTAL TOO?

PRECISELY!

* FOR THE LONG STORY, SEE PAGE 26.

SURF INTO PORTALS

Use library portals to find information about specific subjects and topics. A portal is a website that serves as a point of entry to the Web. It includes links and info that "open doors" to websites about specific topics.

Many libraries now have portals just for teens (see below). You can find info and links about movies, music, relationships, school, sports, and more.

ALL KINDS OF PORTALS:

Look for portals linked on the home page of library websites.
Specific subjects – School subjects like science and history
Local/national history – Unique historical info
News – Links to news and media sources around the world
Careers – Looking for job-search sites? Want to learn how to write a resumé?

HANGING OUT IN TEEN PORTALS

Teen portals created by libraries provide you with useful tools to help with school assignments (and stuff to do when you want to take a break). Links to homework help. Interactive discussion forums. Safe chat rooms.

Teens are also involved with the creation of teen portals. When the Toronto Public Library was working on its portal, RAMP (ramp.torontopubliclibrary.ca), the project team held focus groups with teens, and their input helped shape the website.

Take the time to explore your library's portals and other portals. Here are links to get you started.
YASIG Links (molib.org/yasig/Links.html) – Young Adult Special Interest Group's links to teen sites created by public libraries in the U.S.
Virtual YA Index (yahelp.suffolk.lib.ny.us/virtual.html) – Links to teen sites created by libraries in the U.S. and Canada.

Chat with an electronic librarian
Did you know that you can e-mail and chat with librarians from around the world? So, if you're too shy to approach a librarian in person, look for the "Ask a Librarian" link on library websites (if they have one). This is also a good way to get reliable information on a specific topic from someone in the locale you're interested in. You can only chat during certain hours; when the chat is closed, you can e-mail questions using forms on websites and get a quick reply.

THE GLOBAL LIBRARY NETWORK

Take a look at library websites from around the world. You will be amazed by what you can access from home. For example, the British Library's "Treasures in Full" digital collection (www.bl.uk/treasures/treasuresinfull.html) includes a section on Shakespeare that allows you to view his plays in their original form from the 1600s.

Keep in mind that most library websites don't offer all their resources online. They also usually limit full access to users who have their library cards.

Use a search engine to find these sites. You can also use a directory. Here are two to try:

LibDex: The Library Index (www.libdex.com/country.html) – Links to public, academic, national, and special libraries around the world.

Gabriel (www.bl.uk/gabriel/) – Links to Europe's national libraries. It also highlights special collections and links to their websites.

WHAT'S NEXT?

Now that you have found your information, the hard job's over. Chill out for a bit. When you are ready, you should sort through your notes. Pull out the best information and discard the junk. How? Tune in to the next chapter to learn how to evaluate your information.

Chapter 5

You Be the Judge: What's Good? What's Bad? What's Ugly?

You surf the Web to play games, chat with friends, download songs. When you do, you probably don't stop to think, "I wonder if this website is reliable?"

When you work on school projects, though, it's a little different. Anyone can create a website and post anything they want – but is it credible? So, you should always evaluate your sources. In this chapter, we show you how to do this, as well as how to use diverse sources to soup up your project.

STREET SMARTS FOR CYBERSPACE

People can post outrageous stuff on the Internet, by accident or on purpose (see Zack's story, page 78). It is easy to be deceived if it looks professional. But it's not hard to sort out the good from the bad. Here's what you do.

EVALUATE THE AUTHOR

Did an expert or someone with a unique point of view create the content? Or was it someone with an agenda to promote?
Look for detailed information on the website about the author (or organization).
Why is he or she considered an expert? What information is given about their education and experience?
Find out what other people say about his or her work
(see "Meta-Web search," page 77).

EVALUATE THE CONTENT

Is it the information you need (facts, opinions, interviews)?

Does the website state its aims? Does it deliver on them?

Does the information seem complete and consistent? Does it cover your topic thoroughly or is it advocating a particular bias?

Do you need current information? If so, when was the site last updated?

Do other sources provide better information (for example, books or journals)?

EVALUATE THE LINKS

Does the website link to or offer a list of resources? Do the links work? If not, it means the site is not updated regularly.

Do other websites link to this source (see "Link search," page 79)? What do they have to say?

DO A META-WEB INFORMATION SEARCH

The Media Awareness Network (www.media-awareness.ca) suggests using meta-Web information searches as another way to judge online sources. Use a metasearch engine (see page 34 to remind yourself about metasearch engines) and find out what others say about an author or website.

When you come across a long Web address, you can retype just the first part (everything up to the domain ending) in the address bar. You will arrive at the home page and get a better idea of the purpose of the website's content.

THE BOY WHO BELIEVED THAT THE HOLOCAUST DIDN'T HAPPEN

When Zack's history teacher asked his class to write an essay about a unique topic, Zack decided to write a paper that argued that the Holocaust never happened.

His teacher was shocked. "Zack, where did you hear that the Holocaust didn't happen?" The 14-year-old explained he had found an article on Northwestern University's website titled "A Short Introduction to the Study of Holocaust Revisionism."

The university professor who wrote the article said it was intended for advanced students. It included this paragraph:

During both world wars Germany was forced to fight typhus, carried by lice… That is why all accounts of entry into the German concentration camps speak of shaving of hair and showering and other delousing procedures, such as treatment of quarters with the pesticide Zyklon. *That was also the main reason for a high death rate in the camps* [our italics] …

You're probably wondering how someone could possibly believe that the Holocaust – one of the best-documented events of the 20th century – never happened. But let's look at some of the things that may have misled Zack:

The article's author was a university professor.

It was posted on an official university website.

It was written clearly, with logical arguments and "proof."

If Zack had evaluated his source, however, he would have discovered that:

The professor who wrote the article was an engineering professor. Wouldn't a history professor have been a more appropriate source?

Most universities have an academic-freedom policy that allows professors to write about anything they want.

Scholars and experts have criticized the author of the article, and have labeled him a Holocaust denier.

For Zack, it was an invaluable lesson. His teacher helped him to arrange an interview with a Jewish woman who lived in Europe during World War II (a *primary source*).

As you can see, making the effort to evaluate your sources is just as important as doing the research itself.

Adapted from an article by Alan November that appeared in High School Principal Magazine. You can visit Alan's website at www.novemberlearning.com.

If you see a tilde (~) symbol followed by a name after the domain name of a Web address belonging to an organization or institution (for example, a university), you are likely on a personal Web page. So, the organization might not necessarily support the content and opinions, even if the page is using its domain name. Example: http://www.pretenduniversity.edu/~xander

AUTHOR SEARCH

In the search box, type the author or organization's name in quotation marks (for example, "Madeleine L'Engle"). Your search results may include:

Articles written by the author – What publications are they featured in?

Websites that discuss the author – What do they say?

LINK SEARCH

In the search box, type in "link:" followed by the URL (for example, link:http://msn.foxsports.com). Results will include sites that link to your source.

Are the websites that link to your source credible (for example, educational sites)?

What do they say about your source?

OUTSMARTING ONLINE CHARMERS AND HATERS

Even well-written information can have hidden meanings. You should watch out for ads, propaganda, and hate on the Internet.

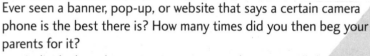
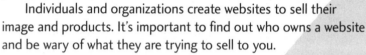

Advertisements

Ever seen a banner, pop-up, or website that says a certain camera phone is the best there is? How many times did you then beg your parents for it?

Individuals and organizations create websites to sell their image and products. It's important to find out who owns a website and be wary of what they are trying to sell to you.

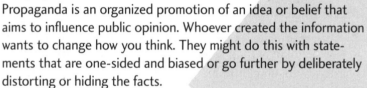

Propaganda

Propaganda is an organized promotion of an idea or belief that aims to influence public opinion. Whoever created the information wants to change how you think. They might do this with statements that are one-sided and biased or go further by deliberately distorting or hiding the facts.

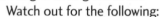

Watch out for the following:

Propaganda uses emotional appeals – personal stories, quotes, photos – as ways to persuade you.

Propaganda favorably presents one viewpoint and disparages others.

Propaganda sites link to online resources that support their statements.

Online Hate/Bullying

Mean-spirited people use the Net to "hate on" others. Some websites want to convince you that white people are superior or that certain types of people are more likely to have HIV/AIDS than others. Your classmates might think it's funny to set up a website to vote on who is the ugliest person in your school.

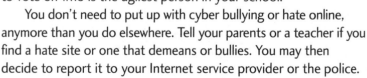

You don't need to put up with cyber bullying or hate online, anymore than you do elsewhere. Tell your parents or a teacher if you find a hate site or one that demeans or bullies. You may then decide to report it to your Internet service provider or the police.

WHERE ON THE WEB ARE YOU? DISSECTING THE URL

It's important to know who created a website and where it was created. To find out, look at the Uniform Resource Locator (URL) – the Web address. The URL is made up of several parts. Consider: http://www.harvard.edu/academics/research.html

Protocol – It indicates how your document is retrieved. "HTTP://" (hypertext transfer protocol) retrieves hypertext documents (most online files are in this format).

www – Short for World Wide Web

Domain (harvard.edu) – It tells you who is hosting the file you are looking at. Read it from right to left. ".edu" is a domain extension (see more below). "harvard" is the domain name.

Document path – This lists the path of directories and sub-directories that lead to the file you are viewing. In this case, it's "academics/".

YOU ARE HERE.

Document name – "research.html" is the name of the file you are viewing.

Domain extensions tell you about who is providing the information.

.com (most cases) – Commercial companies around the world

.org (most cases) – Non-profit organizations around the world

.net (most cases) – Internet companies around the world

Country code – Most countries have their own two-digit country codes. Some also have second-level extensions*. If there is no country code, it usually means that the website is hosted in the United States.

.**au** – Australia　　　.**ca** – Canada
.**cn** – China　　　　　.**fr** – France
.**ru** – Russia　　　　　* .**co.uk** – Commercial site from U.K.

.**gov** – U.S. government bodies (for example, www.whitehouse.gov). Other countries use second-level (or higher) extensions (www.gov.on.ca indicates an Ontario, Canada, government website).

.**edu** – American colleges and universities (www.princeton.edu). Most Canadian universities use .ca (www.utoronto.ca).

STAYING COOL OFFLINE

Non-Internet sources like books, encyclopedias, and journal articles are usually more reliable than Internet ones. Still, you want to use the best information. It's not as hard as it sounds. It's just like evaluating sources on the Internet.

EVALUATE THE BIBLIOGRAPHIC CITATION

Locate the bibliographic citation (in a catalog or database listing, or on a book's copyright page). It is a written description that includes the author, title, publisher, and publication date.
Who is the author? Read his or her biography. How is he or she an expert on the topic (education, work experience)?
What else has he or she written on the topic?
Have you seen his or her name in other sources? Did they have good things to say or bad?
Who is the publisher? For example, university presses or government agencies are considered to be reliable.
When was it published? Is it current or out of date? Does it matter?

EVALUATE THE CONTENT

Look at the summary information (that is, the introduction, table of contents, abstract). Does it match what you are looking for (facts, opinion, interviews, analysis, etc.)? If so, ask the following as you use it:
Is the information well written and well organized?
Looking for facts? If so, is it written in an objective voice or is there bias?
Is it well researched? What evidence does the author provide to support his or her statements?
Can you verify the information in other sources?
Does it cover your topic thoroughly? If not, take a look at other sources.

EVALUATE WHAT OTHERS HAVE SAID

Use a database (newspaper or magazine) or search engine to look for reviews. You can also look in publications like the Book Review Digest. What have others said about your source? Ask librarians or teachers for their opinions, too.

ADDING FLAVOR TO RESEARCH

Your teachers evaluate your research on its accuracy, but they also look at other qualities, like objectivity and flavor. When you use different types of sources, you improve your project's overall quality.

When you're done with the library and Internet, where else can you look?

WHY USE DIFFERENT SOURCES?

Adds credibility – When you have more than one source to support your statements, your argument has more weight.

Adds fairness – When you consider different points of view, it shows that you understand all areas of the issue.

Adds balance – When you pull pieces from different sources into your project, you demonstrate objectivity.

Adds flavor – When you consult more sources, you can find unique or lesser-known facts and quotes.

INTERVIEW PEOPLE

Have you thought about interviewing experts? They can include professors, government officials, members of community or business organizations, and even filmmakers. They might help clarify questions about your research and refer you to more sources. So, how do you find them?

Use a phone or online directory.

Use the Internet and look for their *official* websites.

Ask around, starting with teachers and librarians.

ATTEND GIGS OR ATTRACTIONS

Look at your city's website or newspapers and find out what's happening in your area. When you get there, gather information through interviews, handouts, and observations. Ask organizers if you can take photos. Here are some suggestions.

Local hot spots – Museum? Gallery? Space observatory? Why not take pictures of graffiti on city walls and do a collage of urban art for your art class?

Special events – Look for events like concerts or cultural celebrations. Why not take pictures of a lion dance for a project on Chinese New Year?

Personal appearances – Well-known people often show up at events (for example, a music festival or film screening). Why not attend one and try to interview them?

Library-related events – Ask your librarian or visit the library website to learn about upcoming events. Why not attend a teen author's book reading?

WHAT DOESN'T MAKE THE CUT?

Here's how to decide what gets used or not.

Which info appeals to you? If you don't find it interesting or relevant to your project, others probably won't either.

Which info is unique? Answer all the questions in your topic first. Then add in facts that are less commonly known.

Which info "feels right?" It is often best to go with your instinct.

PUT IT ALL TOGETHER

You are now ready to write your first draft. We briefly discussed how to approach this in Chapter 1. After you complete the draft, you need to do one more important thing: cite your sources. In the next chapter, you'll learn why you should do this and how.

Chapter 6
From APA to MLA: The ABCs of Citing Sources

You've probably heard of classmates who got caught for copying information from a website. Do you know anyone who downloads, buys, or sells essays? This is why schools, colleges, and universities now use anti-plagiarism services, like turnitin.com, to catch students suspected of plagiarism.

What is plagiarism? Your research uses facts and ideas created by someone else. If you don't give credit to these sources by citing them, you are committing plagiarism.

Do you know that even if you take a source and change the words around, you still need to cite it? So, you can even plagiarize without realizing it. The good news is that citing sources is not rocket science. Yes, it may feel like something you'd do in detention, but you have to do it.

You're almost done. You can do it.

WHAT'S YOUR STYLE?
Your teachers probably talk to you about plagiarism and citing sources at the start of every school year. Still, it never hurts to get a little refresher.

You cite sources using different styles. Two common methods are Modern Language Association (MLA) and American Psychological Association (APA). MLA is used for languages, history, and the arts, APA for sciences and math. While the styles are different, they have a lot of similarities:

You insert brief citations within your essay.
You provide a works-cited list at the end of your essay.

There are other styles too – Chicago, Oxford, or Turabian style. Use the style your teacher wants. To keep things simple, you will learn about MLA in this book. You can then ask your teacher or librarian to teach you about other styles. You can also look at the resources listed below.

MLA Handbook for Writers of Research Papers, by Joseph Gibaldi, published by the Modern Language Association of America.

Purdue University Online Writing Lab (OWL) (owl.english. purdue.edu/ handouts/research/) – Learn about MLA, APA, and other styles.

University of Waterloo Electronic Reference (ereference.uwaterloo.ca) – Click on the "Citation and Style Guides" link to learn about many styles.

CREATING IN-ESSAY CITATIONS (NON-INTERNET)

Here's an easy way to remember how to do this. Every time you use a quote, idea, or fact created by someone else, insert a citation (in parentheses) at the end of the sentence.

The citation consists of the author's name and the page number(s) the information is taken from.

The author's name may also appear in your sentence.

If you are using a source that doesn't have page numbers, like a DVD, refer to the author in the sentence. If no author is given, state the title of the source. Some examples:

• "It is our choices, Harry, that show what we truly are, far more than our abilities," said Professor Dumbledore (Rowling 245).

• In the song "Drama Queen (That Girl)," written by Pam Sheyne and Bill Wolfe, Lindsay Lohan sings, "You don't need a high IQ to succeed in what you do ... just believe in yourself."

(See page 90 for more examples of how to insert citations in your essay.)

CREATING A WORKS-CITED LIST (NON-INTERNET)

This is where it gets technical. But it's not as complicated as it looks. You include a works-cited list at the end of your essay. It lists the full bibliographical information for all the sources you've already cited in your essay.

List the sources in alphabetical order by the last name of the author.

List the author by last name, followed by a comma, then first name.

If a source has no author, list it by title.

Take the title of a book from the inside title page, not the cover.

You underline or italicize the titles of your sources, but not both.

Capitalize each word in the title except for *a*, *an*, *the*, or conjunctions such as *and* or *as*.

Indent second and third lines.

So, if you used a book written by a single author, you would use the format below.

Tolkien, J.R.R. <u>Lord of the Rings</u>. New York: Harper Collins, 1991.

(For a complete guide on how to create a works-cited list, see page 90.)

Teacher Cathy Tang says many students don't fully understand what plagiarism is until they do it and get busted. Yes, it sounds like an A+ excuse. Don't try it out though. Ms. Tang recalls that for a music project one Grade 5 student "copied and pasted bits and pieces of biographies of Haydn from five websites, printed it, and slapped on a cover page." What he should have done was a) assimilate the information and then write about Haydn in his own words, and b) put short excerpts of text directly quoted from another source in quotation marks. He should also have cited information he found from other sources in the text and on a works-cited list.

BRAINWAVE

MORE THAN JUST A FAILING MARK

In the working world, the consequences for plagiarism and making up facts (fabrication) are harsh. You can be fired, ruin your reputation, and find it hard to get another job.

In 2003, journalist Jayson Blair resigned from his job at the *New York Times* after accusations of plagiarism.

In a front-page article in the *Times* on May 11 of that year, the editors described how Blair stole material from other news sources. Worse, he often invented facts and quotes. In one five-month period, he invented stories that took place in various cities without being there. He used photos and facts from other sources to create descriptions and told more lies to cover his tracks.

His actions not only destroyed his career, but it also led to the firing of two senior editors. Furthermore, the incident put a black mark on the highly respected *Times*.

After the fiasco, Blair wrote a book in which he blamed his behavior on depression. Even so, is he likely to ever regain the trust of his peers, his editors, or the public?

CREATING IN-ESSAY CITATIONS
(ELECTRONIC SOURCES)

As you did with other sources that don't have page numbers, refer to the author in your sentence. If no author is given, state the name of the website.

• In Anders' online article "Sick Tricks," from *Boys' Life*, skateboard champ Andy Macdonald says that the ollie is an important trick to master because once you know how to do it, you can do the harder tricks.

• SuperBowl.com states that Jerry Rice has scored the most Super Bowl touchdowns in a career, with eight.

CREATING A WORKS-CITED LIST
(ELECTRONIC SOURCES)

You follow guidelines similar to those of non-Internet sources, along with additional ones.

Underline the title of a website or name of a database. If there isn't one, state that it's a Web page (see below).

Don't underline or put the Web page in quotation marks.

You also have to provide the date that you accessed the online source and, if given, when the page was last updated.

List website addresses (URLs) and e-mail addresses in angle brackets, which look like < this >. Don't underline these addresses.

When your citation is more than one line long, divide an address only at a logical place, such as at a slash (/), period, or hyphen (-).

So, if you use an article from the MTV website, you would use the format below.

Reid, Shaheem. "Usher: Souled out." MTV.com. 22 Mar. 2004. MTV Networks. 06 Jan. 2005 <http://www.mtv.com/bands/u/usher /news_feature_031904>.

(For a complete guide on how to create a works-cited list, see page 90.)

DONE. FINITO. SAYONARA!

If you found citing sources a bit tedious, don't sweat it. Trust us, it gets easier with practice.

That's it. You're done. Done! Kick back, Champ. You've earned it.

APPENDIX
Examples of in-essay citations and works-cited lists for various media, following **Modern Language Association (MLA)** guidelines.

INSERTING CITATIONS WITHIN YOUR ESSAY (NON-INTERNET)
Single author
If you use the author's name in your sentence, you need only the page number in your citation.
Shari Graydon reports that three years after American television was introduced into Fiji, 15% of girls had tried vomiting to lose weight (34).

Multiple authors
The names of two authors are joined by "and." When you have three or more authors, use the first author's last name, followed by "et al."
(Shulman and Krog 41) or (Jones et al. 227)

Long quotations
To quote information longer than four lines, start the quotation on a new line, making sure you indent. Don't use quotation marks. Your citation comes at the end.
In a scene from Fahrenheit 451, Faber notes to Montag:
> Books were only one type of receptacle where we stored a lot of things we were afraid we might forget. There is nothing magical in them at all. The magic is only in what books say, how they stitched the patches of the universe together into one garment for us. (Bradbury 83)

Source within a source
Use the abbreviation "qtd. in" if you are citing a source found within another source.
In a letter to an American correspondent, George Orwell writes that he doesn't believe the society he describes in *1984* will necessarily arrive, but he believes that something resembling it could arrive (qtd. in Howe 18).

Plays
Cite the author name, page number, act and scene (if any).
As Blanche exits at the end of A Streetcar Named Desire, she notes, "I have always depended on the kindness of strangers" (Tennessee Williams 147; act 1 scene 11).

CREATING A WORKS-CITED LIST (NON-INTERNET)
Note: If you can't find information like author name or edition number, leave it blank and cite the available information in the same order as if the missing information were there.

Books
Author(s). Title of Book. Edition (if any). City of Publication: Publisher, Year of Publication.

One author
Toronto Public Library. Research Ate My Brain: The Panic-Proof Guide to Surviving Homework. Toronto: Annick Press, 2005.

Two authors
Yolen, Jane and Bruce Coville. Armageddon Summer. San Diego: Harcourt Brace + Company, 1998.

Multiple works by the same author
Oppel, Kenneth. Sunwing. New York: Aladdin, 2001.
—. The Devil's Cure. New York: Hyperion, 2002.

Three or more authors
Cunningham, William P. et al. Environmental Science: A Global Concern. 7th ed. New York: McGraw Hill, 2003.

Editor
Armstrong, Jennifer, ed. Shattered: Stories of Children and War. New York: Knopf, 2001.

Essays, poems or short stories from a collection
Author of piece. "Title of Piece." Title of Book. Editor. Edition (if any). City of Publication: Publisher, Year. Page(s).
Stevenson, Robert Louis. "The Body Snatcher." Classic Ghost Stories: Eighteen Spine-Chilling Tales of Terror and the Supernatural. Ed. Bill Bowers. Guilford: The Lyons Press, 2003. 175-205

Encyclopedias and reference books
Author(s). "Title of article." Title of Book. Edition. City of Publication: Publisher, Year.
"Ballet." World Book Student Discovery Encyclopedia. Chicago: World Book, Inc., 2003.

Newspapers
Author(s). "Title of Article." Title of Newspaper Day Month Year, edition (if included): Page(s).
Curtiss, Aaron. "Resident Evil 3 Full of Terror and Fun." Los Angeles Times 2 Dec. 1999: C6.

Note: For news and magazine articles, list the first and last page numbers separated by a dash if the page numbers are consecutive (ex. 136-145). If they are not consecutive, write down the first page number followed by a plus sign (ex. write 136, 143, 157 as 136+)

Journals
Author(s). "Title of Article." Title of Journal Volume Number.Issue Number (Year): Page(s).
Mattson, Kevin. "Did Punk Matter?: Analyzing the Practices of a Youth Subculture During the 1980s." American Studies 42.1 (2001): 69-97.

Video recordings
Title. Credits (Director, Producer, Writer, etc.) Medium. Distributor, Date.
Spider-Man 2. Dir. Sam Raimi. DVD. Columbia Tri-Star, 2004.

Interviews you conducted
Person Interviewed. Type of Interview (phone, e-mail, etc.). Day Month Year.
Sandler, Adam. Phone Interview. 14 Feb. 2005.

CREATING A WORKS-CITED LIST (ELECTRONIC SOURCES)
Entire website
Title of website. Date of last update. Name of organization. Access Date <URL>.
The White House. 08 May 2005. The White House. 08 May 2005 <www.whitehouse.gov>.

Individual Web pages
Author. "Title of Web page." Title of the website. Date of last update. Name of organization. Access Date <URL>.
"Tours." The White House. 07 Feb. 2005. The White House. 08 May 2005 <http://www.whitehouse.gov/kids/tours>.

Online newspaper articles
Author. "Title of Article." Title of Newspaper Day Month Year. Access Date <URL>.
"Tortoise Adopts Stray Hippo at Sanctuary." Reuters 06 Jan. 2005. 07 Jan. 2005 <http://story.news. yahoo. com/news?tmpl=story&cid= 583&ncid=583&e=8&u=/nm/ 20050106/od_nm/ kenya_hippo_dc>.

Articles from library databases
Author. "Title of Article." Original Source of Article Date of original source: Page Numbers. Name of database. Name of service. Name of library. Access Date <URL>.
"Zimbabwe: Youth Provide Leadership for AIDS Effort." Africa News Service 20 May 2004. Expanded Academic ASAP. Gale. Toronto Public Library. 29 Dec. 2004 <http://www .galegroup.com>.

GLOSSARY

Abstract A statement that summarizes the main points of a larger body of text.

Bibliographic citation A source's written description that includes the author, title, and publication information.

Citation A reference to or quotation of a source to provide evidence of research.

Classification system The method of using numbers and alphabets to organize library materials on the shelves in a logical manner (e.g., Dewey Decimal Classification System).

Database A collection of data that can be easily searched for and retrieved.

Deep Web Information on the Internet that is not readily retrieved using regular search engines. It is also referred to as the Invisible Web.

Digital collection Electronic collection that features materials such as books and newspapers scanned in their original form into an electronic format.

Directory A book or electronic resource that contains a classified listing of names, addresses, and other data.

Domain name The unique name identifying an Internet site.

Frequently Asked Questions (FAQ) A document created to answer common questions.

HyperText Transfer Protocol (HTTP) The way in which Web pages are sent through the Internet.

Index An alphabetical list that helps guide, point out, and facilitate reference.

Journal A **periodical** presenting peer-reviewed articles on a particular subject.

Metasearch engine A **search engine** that searches more than one search engine at a time.

Periodical A body of text published at regular intervals of more than one day.

Plagiarism The act of taking another person's work and passing it off as one's own.

Plug-in Software program, often used with a Web browser, required to open certain types of files.

Portal A website that serves as an entryway to other websites, usually of a specific topic. Also referred to as a gateway.

Primary source Sources of information that have been created firsthand and usually close to the time an event has occurred, such as an interview, diary, or original research report.

Reference A work that is frequently used as a source for research. In many libraries, reference materials are often for use in the library only.

Search engine A program used to search for information on the World Wide Web.

Secondary source A source of information created based on information found in primary sources.

Subject directory An online search tool that allows you to do subject searches or browse an index to find websites that have been selected by experts.

Uniform Resource Locator (URL) The addressing system used on the World Wide Web.

Works-cited list A list of sources used or considered by an author in preparing a particular work.

World Wide Web (WWW) A computer network – created by Tim Berners-Lee – that consists of Web pages, graphics, sound, and animation resources available through a browser.

FURTHER READING

What else can you research?
Research is a lifelong skill that you improve upon through practice. The library and online tools you learned about in this book can be applied for other purposes.

Prepare for college and university
Look at larger libraries for the calendars of colleges and universities, or use a search engine to find their websites. These sites offer information on programs, student life, admission policies, athletics, student exchanges and more.

Study for the SAT and TOEFL
The SAT is a standardized entrance exam that colleges and universities in the United States give to select their successful applicants. The Test of English as a Foreign Language (TOEFL) measures the ability of non-native English speakers to use and understand North American English.

Libraries usually carry study guides for both tests. For useful online resources, use a search engine or look at school and library websites for links. Here are two:
Free SAT Prep (www.freesat1prep.com)
TestMagic TOEFL Page (www.testmagic.com/toefl)

Consult college and university rankings
Find out what other experts and students have to say about the schools you're interested in. Ask your librarian about the following:
U.S. News and World Report **College Rankings and University Rankings**
The magazine's annual edition ranks U.S. colleges and universities on topics like acceptance rates and campus life. (www.usnews.com).
Maclean's **Annual University Rankings** – The magazine's annual edition ranks Canadian universities on similar topics. (www.macleans.ca/universities /index.jsp).

Looking for jobs, work-abroad opportunities, volunteer work, or interested in developing job skills? Some websites to check out:
Studentjobs.gov (www.studentjobs.gov) (U.S.)
Cool Works (www.coolworks.com) (U.S.)
workopolisCampus (campus.workopolis.com) (Canadian)
Youth at the United Nations (www.un.org/youth)
TakingITGlobal (www.takingitglobal.org) (International)

The world at your fingertips
Now that you know how to find reliable and useful information, there really isn't anything that you can't research at your library or on the Internet.

WORKS CITED

Unless otherwise stated, the information in this book was drawn from the Toronto Public Library's resources.

CHAPTER 1
"Primary and Secondary Sources." Joyner Library Academic Library Services. East Carolina University. 05 May 2005 <http://www.lib.ecu.edu/Reference /workshop/primary.html>.

"Primary Sources vs. Secondary Sources." Bergen Community College. 03 Aug. 04. Bergen Community College. 05 May 2005 <http://www.bergen.cc.nj .us/Library /userguide/IV_A_prim _sec.html>.

Shenton, Andrew K. and Pat Dixon. "Issues Arising From Youngsters' Information-Seeking Behavior." Library and Information Science Research 26.2 (2004): 177-200.

CHAPTER 2
Dewey, Melvil. Dewey Decimal Classification and Relative Index. Ed. Joan S. Mitchell et al. 22nd ed. Vol. 2. Ohio: OCLC Online Computer Library Center, 2003.

"Library of Congress Classification Outline." The Library of Congress. The Library of Congress. 05 May 2005 <http://www.loc.gov/catdir/ cpso/lcco/lcco.html>.

Prytherch, Ray. Harrod's Librarians' Glossary and Reference Book. 9th ed. Vermont: Gower, 2000.

CHAPTER 3
"Deep Web FAQ." BrightPlanet. 2005. BrightPlanet Corporation. 6 May 2005 <http://www.brightplanet .com/ deepcontent/deep_web_faq.asp>.

Gil, Paul. "Plug-Ins 101." About.com. About, Inc. 05 May 2005 <http:// netforbeginners.about.com/cs/ multimedia/a/plugins101.htm? terms=Plug-Ins>.

"Internet." Encyclopaedia Britannica Online. 2004. Encyclopaedia Britannica, Inc. 13 Dec. 2004 <http://www.search.eb.com/eb /article?tocId=9001458>.

Sherman, Chris and Gary Price. "The Invisible Web." Searcher June 2001: 62+.Computer Database. Gale. Toronto Public Library. 05 May 2005 <http://www.galegroup.com>.

Sullivan, Danny. "Search Engine Math." Search Engine Watch. 26 Oct. 2001. Jupitermedia Corporation. 05 May 2005 <http://searchenginewatch. com/facts/article.php/2156021>.

"The Deep Web." University at Albany. 06 Dec. 2004. University at Albany. 05 May 2005 <http://library.albany .edu/internet/deepweb.html>.

CHAPTER 5
"Authenticating Online Information." Media Awareness Network. Media Awareness Network. 05 May 2005 <http://www.media-awareness.ca /english/resources/special _initiatives /wa_resources/wa_shared /tipsheets /quick_tips_authenticating.cfm>.

Engle, Michael. "How to Evaluate the Information Sources You Find." Cornell University Library Gateway. 31 Mar. 2004. Cornell University Library. 05 May 2005 <http://www .library.cornell.edu/olinuris/ref /research/evaluate.html>.

"Evaluating Sources of Information." Purdue University's Online Writing Lab. OWL at Purdue University and Purdue University. 05 May 2005 <http://owl.english.purdue.edu /handouts/research/r_evalsource .html>.

"Evaluating Web Pages: Techniques to Apply & Questions to Ask." University of California Berkeley Library. The Regents of the University of California. 05 May 2005 <http://www.lib.berkeley.edu/TeachingLib/Guides/Internet/Evaluate.html>.

"Five W's of Cyberspace." Media Awareness Network. Media Awareness Network. 05 May 2005 <http://www.media-awareness.ca/english/resources/special_initiatives/wa_resources/wa_shared/tipsheets/5Ws_of_cyberspace.cfm>.

November, Alan. "Teaching Zack to Think." November Learning. November Learning. 05 May 2005 <http://www.anovember.com/articles/zack.html>.

"OWL at Purdue University: Evaluating Internet Sources." Purdue University's Online Writing Lab. OWL at Purdue University and Purdue University. 05 May 2005 <http://owl.english.purdue.edu /handouts/research/r_evalsource4 .html>.

CHAPTER 6

Anders, Mark. "Sick Tricks: Skateboard Champ Andy Macdonald Shows These Scouts—and You!—How to Skate Like a Pro." Boys' Life August 2003: 14-19. General Reference Center Gold. Gale. Toronto Public Library. 05 May 2005 <http://www.galegroup.com>.

Lohan, Lindsay. "Drama Queen (That Girl)." By Pam Sheyne and Bill Wolfe. Confessions of a Teenage Drama Queen (Soundtrack). Hollywood, 2004.

Rowling, J.K. Harry Potter and the Chamber of Secrets. Vancouver: Raincoast Books, 1999.

"Super Bowl Records." SuperBowl.com. 2005. NFL Enterprises LLC. 05 May 2005 <http://www.superbowl.com/history/records/indiv/touchdowns>.

"Times Reporter Who Resigned Leaves Long Trail of Deception." The New York Times 11 May 2003: A1+.

APPENDIX

Gibaldi, Joseph. MLA Handbook for Writers of Research Papers. 6th ed. New York: The Modern Language Association of America, 2003.

● ●

ACKNOWLEDGMENTS

This amazing learning opportunity would not have been possible without the support of the Toronto Public Library and Annick Press.

A million thanks to: Ken Setterington for your guidance, the people at Annick for your belief in me, Martha Newbigging and Sheryl Shapiro for making the book look so nice, and Carolyn Kennedy for being an encouraging and super editor.

Thanks to the following for their help: Brian Bertrand, Debbie Childs, Anna Cocca, Patricia Eastman, John Elmslie, Helen Flint, Norma Grech, Beatriz Hausner, Joanne Hawthorne, Lisa Heggum, Phyllis Jacklin, Greg Kelner, Ranald Krolman, Ellen Lewkowicz, Haney Mussa, Elsa Ngan, Peggy Perdue, Ann Rauhala, Cathy Tang, Gloria Whyte, Sue Young, and the YAG members who participated in our focus groups. Special thanks go to the ever-helpful Sharon Moynes, Dorota Rajewska, and the TPL Foundation staff.

Lastly, thanks to my family, friends, and Andrew Thibideau for the laughs during the times when research did almost eat my brain.

—Ab. Velasco

To Liam and Eli, my drawing pen pals.

—M.N.

INDEX